BEGINNING T

A practical guide to preaching well

Foreword by
The Archbishop of Canterbury

Robert Beaken

TUFTON
B O O K S

First published in 2004 by Tufton Books (Church Union Publications)
In conjunction with
Canterbury Press Norwich, a division of Hymns Ancient & Modern Ltd
(a registered charity), St Mary's Works, St Mary's Plain,
Norwich, Norfolk NR3 3BH

Reprinted 2005

Bible quotations are from the Revised Standard Version

British Library Cataloguing in Publication Data.

A catalogue record for this book is available from the British Library.

ISBN   0-85191-047-5

Printed in Great Britain by The Bidnall Press Ltd, Beccles, Suffolk

CONTENTS

FOREWORD BY
DR ROWAN WILLIAMS
ARCHBISHOP OF CANTERBURY

Reading these lively, practical and wise pages, I found myself asking again and again why no one had put all this down on paper with such clarity years ago. Preaching is still - and rightly - so central a task for the Church's ministers that it is really extraordinary that we have so little in the way of clear written guidance (and let no-one say that preaching is dead as a means of communication; it remains a unique and remarkably welcome aspect of the life of every church of whatever tradition). Father Beaken has been give the rare grace of hearing a simple question clearly and answering it honestly.

What is so good about this little book is that it is really about *sermons*. My heart sinks when I hear yet another address that is a loose amalgam of autobiography, newspaper commentary and general uplift. Father Beaken begins by insisting that you first ask what God wants you to say to these people here and now about this bit of the Bible. The newspaper and the autobiography may or may not come in handy later on - but you have to begin, soberingly, by asking about the will of God and the self-revelation of God. If you don't believe in that self-revelation, you may produce a more or less interesting talk about religion or the Meaning of Life; but you won't be preaching.

i

The good news is that if you really try to keep that basic question before you and do your best, God will say something, even if your sermon isn't up to much in itself. The not-so-good news is, of course, that a polished and eloquent performance may be neither here nor there in God's purposes if all it does is direct attention to the preacher. We've all experienced this - the beautifully crafted discourse that meets with blank looks, the sermon we feel is muddled and banal as we preach it, but which stirs someone to come and say that you've changed their life. One of my recurring fantasies when preaching a sermon that isn't 'connecting' is of being surrounded in the pulpit by a glass wall: the words go out, hit the wall and drop down to the ground, so that by the end of the sermon there is a little pile of dead words under the pulpit. For the glass wall to be lowered, both preacher and people need to be in a state of expectation that God is involved here: expectation that my words will be carried forward on the powerful tide of God's Word, God's self-communication in Jesus, in Bible and sacraments, so that a real *communion* occurs.

I hope others will feel as they read these pages that this is a book they have been waiting for. Consistently sensible and sensitive, covering all sorts of situations, and above all grounded in a clear conviction about what a sermon theologically is, this is a treasure of a book, which should be read by every ministerial student at every level, as well as by practitioners up to and including Archbishops.

✠ Rowan Cantuar

1.   INTRODUCTION

"How do you preach?" The question was unexpected and caught me off guard. I had been looking at some Biblical commentaries in a bookshop with an ordinand about to begin training at theological college and his mind moved from the Bible to sermons. I replied that one began with the appointed readings from the Bible and prayed about them, asking God for guidance and inspiration. I was conscious as the words passed my lips that this reply was hardly very helpful to him. The question 'how do you preach?' whirled around my head all afternoon and when I returned home that evening I sat down and began to type-up some notes for him on preaching, sermon preparation and delivery. This little booklet is based upon those notes.

I confess that I enjoy preaching but that I am also very challenged by it. The preacher's art straddles prayer, theology in its various areas, pastoral care, common sense, literature, voice control, self-discipline, and includes a touch of the theatre. Looking back at my time at theological college, the kindest thing one could say about my training in preaching is that it was extremely sketchy. I am eternally grateful that one of the parish priests to whom I was a curate was a very fine and gifted preacher. I learnt much from listening to him in the pulpit and from discussions at our staff meetings. What follows is based upon observation, reflection, and trial and error over the past sixteen years. It is offered as a little guide for beginners to ordinands, clergy, readers, members of religious communities and all who are called to the ministry of the word, in the hope that it may spark off some ideas and encourage them for the important and exciting work before them.

2.   PREACHING

Two ideas undergird all that follows. The first is the belief that the primary purposes for which the Church of God exists on earth are to worship Almighty God, to tell people about His Son Jesus Christ, and to work out the implications of Christ's incarnation, life, teaching, crucifixion and resurrection in the life of the present generation. Everything else the Church does is of secondary importance. We are in the business of communicating the Good News by many different means and I firmly believe in the importance of preaching in church Sunday by Sunday as a central part of this task. Good preaching will not by itself necessarily attract people to church or commend Christianity to them, but bad preaching will surely drive them away and dispirit already existing churchgoers. I would add to this my conviction that the principal Sunday service ought to be the Eucharist with a sermon, because word and sacrament go together.

Secondly, I believe that the bulk of preaching on Sundays ought to be Biblical, i.e. based upon the readings appointed for that day in a lectionary. The canonical scriptures of the Old and New Testaments are the uniquely inspired word of God, given to us by the Holy Spirit for our guidance and nourishment during our earthly pilgrimage to God. It seems silly to read two or three portions of scripture in church and then not to preach about them. The prayer on the lips of every preacher week by week ought to be *"Lord, what do you want me to say about this passage of scripture to these people?"*

What would I say, though, to those whose idea of Biblical preaching might be to choose themselves a portion of Scripture each week upon which to preach or to work through a book of the Bible, taking a few verses each Sunday? It is no bad thing *occasionally* to depart from the appointed readings and to select your own readings if you have a special service, but the danger with simply choosing your own readings as a matter of course is that you can end up selecting the same favourite or easy passages over and over again. The careful, consecutive preaching of sermons based upon the appointed readings will provide a varied spiritual diet and also prevent the preacher from constantly returning to half a dozen pet subjects or hobby horses.

I am a little happier with working through a book of the Bible verse by verse which at least has the merit of consistency, but in the wrong hands it can be rather dull and is not the ideal way to preach regularly at the Eucharist. We are also members of a Church with a liturgical tradition which appoints a course of readings in a lectionary for us to use throughout the year. I have sometimes found that the appointed readings have had an uncanny knack of speaking to me when I have been faced with problems or had to deal with difficult issues: it is as though certain words in the text have been printed in red ink instead of black and have leapt off the page at me. Those readings were appointed by a committee months if not years ago, and yet they are fresh and relevant to my present needs and I would probably never have found them if I had simply leafed through the Bible. One concludes that the Holy Spirit must in some way - though not exclusively so - work through the lectionary.

It is important to bear this in mind when one is confronted with some particularly hard readings in the lectionary and not take the easy way out by preaching on that Sunday about the parish's need of a new church hall.

3. SERMONS AND CONGREGATIONS

When planning a sermon it is important to think carefully about both the type of service at which you will be preaching and also the sort of people who will be in the congregation to listen to you.

Just as there are a wide variety of different church services, so there are a variety of forms of preaching. An address at Compline on a weekday evening during Lent, for instance, is quite different to a talk during a Christingle service on Christmas Eve. The former will tend to be devotional, delivered in measured tones and will seek to leave a few thoughts to be pondered in the minds of the congregation. The latter will be attention-grabbing, brief ('quit while you are winning' is good advice at children's services), easily understandable, and loud in order to get over the noise of excited children and their baby brothers and sisters. Sermons at the Eucharist will be governed by the Church's year, the liturgical occasion and the readings in the lectionary. Much the same is true of Matins and Evensong. Sermons on Good Friday, to take an obvious example, will be sombre and serious, whilst on Easter Day or at Pentecost they will be joyful.

How long do you think your sermon should last? When I went to church as a boy in the 1970s the sermon usually lasted twenty or twenty-five minutes and forty minutes was not unknown. People's attention spans have diminished over the years, in part due to the influence of television. A good, short sermon making one point crisply is far better than a long, rambling one making three rather blurry points, but a concise sermon takes more thought and preparation.

If you are preaching at the 8.00 a.m. Eucharist on Sunday - or at a weekday celebration - you might wish to preach for no more than two or three minutes, especially if time is of the essence. Some preachers deliver a shortened version at 8.00 a.m. of the sermon they will be preaching in full later on Sunday morning (it may help to place a red line down the left margin to indicate which parts of the text are to be preached at 8.00 a.m.) Other people deliver the same sermon in full at both 8.00 a.m. and the principal Sunday Eucharist.

If you are preaching at a Sung Eucharist with a mixed congregation of adults and children I would suggest that you should *aim* to preach for five minutes, which means you will probably go on for seven or eight. You should certainly preach for no longer than five minutes if you have a Baptism as part of your Sung Eucharist. Sermons at Matins and Evensong may perhaps be a little longer, though sermons at Family Services and services for children should be quite brief and to the point.

Who will be in the congregation when you preach? What is appropriate in a church attracting lots of students in a university town will not always be appropriate in an urban priority area parish or in a remote village church and vice versa. The preacher needs to understand the anxieties and concerns of the congregation in order to help them. It is always useful to read a local newspaper or to watch the local television news. Has anyone in the congregation recently suffered a tragedy, accident or bereavement? The way you chose the topic for your sermon or handle it may be affected by the answer. A sermon on the aorist tense in the Greek text of St John's Gospel (I am not joking!) will not be of much comfort to a suburban congregation suffering a spate of sudden redundancies or to an agricultural congregation devastated by foot and mouth disease.

The preacher should be aware that within a church the composition of the congregation will vary a good deal throughout the year: on the Fourteenth Sunday after Trinity the pews will probably mostly contain regular worshippers, whilst at the great festivals of the Church's year and at events such as Harvest Thanksgiving and Remembrance Sunday the congregation is likely to include a number of strangers or newcomers to the district. We are apt to forget that regular churchgoers have absorbed a Christian vocabulary and ways of thinking which they then take for granted but which are unfamiliar and perhaps off-putting to those venturing into church for the first time or after a long absence. How will our sermon be intelligible to both regular worshippers and newcomers?

4.   PREPARING A SERMON

The preacher is God's messenger. The aim of sermon preparation is to discern what God wants you to say. Careful preparation is essential to a good sermon: no matter how brilliant your oratorical skills, if there is no clear message at the heart of your sermon it will be no more than entertaining froth.

On Monday morning read the readings appointed in the lectionary for the following Sunday and let them stew around in your head for a few days. Remember that the first idea to occur to you for a sermon may not always be the best or the most appropriate. You might find it helpful to look up the readings in several different versions of the Bible. If you understand Hebrew or Greek you might wish to look up the readings in the Hebrew Old Testament or the Greek New Testament. An interlinear Greek-English New Testament can be very helpful to those of us whose Greek has become a bit rusty. Look, too, at the position of the text: what precedes or follows it in that book from the Bible? It might also be prudent to look at the next Sunday's readings because if they are a continuation of the text and are dealing with a similar topic you do not want to use up all your ideas one week and then struggle for something to say the next.

By about Wednesday begin looking up the readings in a commentary. Few of us will have a commentary on every book of the Bible. A good one-volume commentary such as *The Oxford Bible Commentary, Peake's Commentary* or *The New Jerome Commentary* will give you a basic overview. It is a good idea to build up a little collection of more detailed commentaries on the four Gospels and perhaps some of the other books of the Bible. You may also find it useful to obtain a good concordance to help you find passages of scripture. Keep an eye out for old Biblical commentaries and books of old sermons in second-hand bookshops: our scholarship may have moved on and styles of preaching have changed over the years but we can still learn a lot from the insights of older writers. I have found the *Catena Aurea*, St Thomas Aquinas' compendium of comments on the Gospels from the writings of the Fathers, to be very helpful in sparking off trains of thought. Look up the background to the Bible reading in books about the Holy Land and about life in ancient Israel or at the time of Christ. H.V. Morton's *In the Steps of the Master* has recently been reissued in paperback and is a good source of colourful background material. Look out for his other works, *Through the Lands of the Bible* and *In the Steps of St Paul* in second-hand bookshops, which are also of great help.

Find time to pray quietly about the readings, and, as I said earlier, ask God what He wants you to say about these readings in your sermon. When it is not unbearably cold I sometimes sit in the Lady Chapel in front of the reserved sacrament in the tabernacle, absorbing the special sense of peace and quiet. I take my Bible and books with me, read them quietly and have a little chat with Jesus. It is surprising what ideas one gets given. A particular text may seem awful at first but after a while spent in prayer a very good idea occurs for a sermon. Conversely, one may hurriedly prepare a sermon on a well-known and easy passage of scripture but it is a flop when one preaches it because one has not spent enough time in preparation.

An older custom and one still worth bearing in mind is that of preaching a course of sermons on a particular theme on several successive Sundays, e.g. on the Four Last Things (death, judgement, heaven and hell) on the four Sundays of Advent, the Ten Commandments during Lent, the sacraments during Eastertide, or about the Lord's Prayer, the Creed, or other key parts of Christianity at other times during the year. It is helpful if you can relate the appointed readings in the lectionary to your theme but this is not always possible and you may wish to make use of other portions of scripture. On other occasions you should try to preach about the appointed readings.

The tradition of expository sermons - taking a passage of scripture and working your way through it line by line, sometimes word by word - has largely fallen into disuse except in some evangelical parishes. This sort of sermon is generally more suited for preaching to regular churchgoers than to newcomers to Christianity. I have had some success with expository addresses at Compline and have sometimes included a much-disguised expository element in some sermons preached at the Eucharist. It is helpful if the congregation can have the passage of scripture in front of them to refer to from time to time, but the preacher should remember that a sermon is not the same as a seminar on the Bible.

It is customary - though not graven in tablets of stone - to preach on the Gospel at the Eucharist because the Gospel is in a sense the high point of the readings. The Old Testament prepares the way for the Gospels with their accounts of the words and deeds of Christ and it sometimes furnishes some point which Jesus reacts against (*"You have heard it said 'an eye for an eye, a tooth for a tooth'. But I say to you, Do not resist one who is evil. But if anyone strikes you on the right cheek, turn him the other also"*, etc.), whilst the Epistles are reflections on the Good News. At other services you can preach on any of the readings.

Since the Second Century AD when Marcion produced a heretical version of Christianity which repudiated the Old Testament, the Church has been keen to stress that the New Testament flows out of the Old Testament and that Christ is the fulfilment of the Law. As Monsignor Ronald Knox once observed, 'The Old Testament is the lock into which fits the key of the Incarnation', yet in how many churches is there a diet of sermons based upon the New Testament with only the most passing mention of the Old Testament background?

5. WRITING A SERMON

By about Thursday you should be ready to begin writing your sermon. Before you start, try to sum up in as few words as possible - ideally a single sentence - what you want your hearers to take away with them in their minds. You might find it helpful to write this on a slip of paper and to have it in front of you so you can refer to it from time to time and see how your sermon is matching up to it - or not. If you cannot express the central idea of your sermon in just a few words there is little chance that the congregation will be able to remember much of it afterwards. This habit will be reinforced if you make an entry in the 'Subject' column of the Register of Services, to the right of the column for the preacher's signature, e.g. *'The Holy Spirit points us to Jesus'*, *'Miracle of loaves and fishes prepares the way for the Last Supper'*, etc.

I would suggest that you write or print your sermon on white paper using black ink and fairly large letters, though some dyslexics find yellow paper helpful. It is very embarrassing when the preacher has written his sermon in tiny letters on a small piece of paper or in pencil on the back of an old brown envelope and keeps losing his way because he cannot see to read in a badly illuminated church. Many people use A4 paper but the reading desks in old pulpits - especially if they are fitted with an electric light at the front - are often constructed for much smaller pieces of paper. You may have to try A5 paper, which has the added advantage that it is less difficult to lose your place on A5 paper than on A4. Write on one side only of your paper and number the sheets clearly.

Please do not leave preparing your sermon until Saturday, which is often a busy day in a parish. You would be surprised what you can manage in a hurry, but the Lord is worth more than this. Most of the hard work with preaching is done at your desk. You may have to prepare two sermons in one week. I would suggest that you look at the readings for both sermons at the start of the week and let them ferment in your head for a few days. You will then need to prioritise the sermons: a sermon for a Sung Eucharist with a large congregation should have priority over a sermon for a handful of people at Evensong. You should write the more important sermon first but have a deadline in mind by which to finish it and begin writing the second sermon. You might, for instance, aim to finish the first sermon by Thursday evening and the second by Friday evening.

Like a good novel or a good play, a good sermon has a clear beginning, middle and end. You must get the attention of your hearers as soon as you open your mouth. *"Cor! That dog stinks!" said my four-year-old son when we met the Queen walking her Corgis:* everyone wants to know what is coming next? If you start weakly and the congregation begins to think about lunch or taking the car for its M.O.T., you have largely lost your opportunity. The congregation may give you their attention if you say something that disturbs their reverie but they will probably not remember very much and may get the wrong end of the stick.

Stories in sermons always go down well especially with children or congregations containing people unaccustomed to going to church. Jesus used stories to convey very deep and subtle teaching in an understandable and memorable way. The story must be relevant, though: we have all sat through sermons which have been mostly story with an inadequate little point tacked onto the end. Do not be afraid to remind people about things they already know but may have pushed to the back of their minds.

Try to keep your sentences simple: they will be more easily understood and you will be less likely to stumble over your words when preaching them. Do not always say *'you'* in your sermon because this can seem to imply that *'you'* are different or inferior to *'me'*, which is most certainly not the case. Try instead to include yourself by saying *'we'*, though there may be occasions when it is preferable to risk sticking with *'you'* in order to avoid clumsy or unnatural English.

In sermons addressed to mixed congregations try to slip in the occasional reference to children to let them know that your words include them as well as the grown-ups, e.g. *'Jesus promises forgiveness of sins and a fresh start to all men and women, boys and girls.'*

Sometimes the preacher will have to say hard or difficult things in a sermon. Pray particularly carefully when preparing your sermon and try to say whatever it is in a nice way. Avoid sweeping statements which might inadvertently cause offence. Make a point of including yourself in your sermon, e.g. *'I expect that like me you've said things in the heat of the moment which you wish you could take back.'* Remember, it is better to exhort someone to do better for the Lord in the future than it is to condemn all he or she has done up until now.

Never use your sermon to 'get' at a member of the congregation or to single someone out for praise (unless it is something such as a golden wedding). The pulpit is not the place for vendettas or to settle old scores. Although it is appropriate for the preacher to look from a Christian perspective at issues of the day and political questions such as unemployment, terrorism or the current international situation, Party politics are best kept out of the pulpit unless the circumstances are exceptionally grave. One example of the latter might be the preacher in Birmingham who looked at some of the issues surrounding extremist candidates in a sermon preached shortly before a local election.

Do not parade your learning from the pulpit. We need preachers who understand Theology and Biblical Criticism and who will remember what they learnt during their training, but we do not need preachers who show off in front of the congregation. It should also be remembered that a sermon is not the same as a lecture. It is a very good idea to review from time to time the subjects you have covered in your sermons to see what areas you are missing out or not covering very well.

The question of humour in the sermon is rather a delicate one. A humorous remark can catch the attention of the congregation and help them to relax so they can begin to hear what you have to say. Humour can heal and unite and there are humorous passages in the Bible. Yet the preacher should remember that he is not a comedian and his service is not a comedy turn: a series of gags every Sunday will soon start to pall. Yet, a preacher with no sense of humour, irony, or the ability to have a good laugh at him or her self must be a very dull creature.

There is no reason why you should not give personal opinion in a sermon, so long as you make it quite clear that this is what it is: "My personal view on this point is..." After all, you are not primarily in the pulpit to give your own opinions but to nourish and guide the people of God. For this reason, although it is now considered a bit old-fashioned (trendy preachers just get up and talk, with nothing special at the beginning or end), I like to begin and end my sermons with a Trinitarian ascription: 'In the name of the Father, and of the Son, and of the Holy Spirit. Amen'. Although it might be objected that all Christian worship is Trinitarian and not just the sermon, this traditional ascription makes it quite clear who is ultimately supposed to be speaking in the sermon. In some churches it is instead the tradition to begin and end sermons with a prayer, which makes the same point in a different way.

Finally, give your sermon a definite and clear ending, perhaps with a few sentences or a quotation which sum up all that you have been saying (refer back to the slip of paper with the sentence summing up what you want your congregation to remember afterwards to help you), or possibly with a question for the congregation to take home and think about. At all costs avoid a sermon which just seems to peter out.

When you have finished, put your sermon away and go and do something completely different. Take it out again the next day, read it and make any changes that seem necessary.

6. EXTEMPORE SERMONS

Extempore sermons are when the preacher preaches without written text. Some people have this gift, others only think they have. I have sometimes preached extempore sermons, or perhaps preached with a few headings on a little slip of paper to remind me of the main points I want to get across.

The danger with extempore sermons is (1) you repeat yourself and waffle, (2) you get carried away with your own train of thought and say something over the top, and (3) you can easily be put off and lose your thread so that you flounder, perhaps by a door slamming, the arrival of latecomers, a crying baby, a member of the congregation walking out. You will wonder if he or she is in search of a drink of water? The lavatory? Or are they upset by something you've said? This will not help your concentration.

It must be said that extempore sermons are much harder if the preacher is feeling under the weather: if you have been ill during Saturday night or are bravely coming to church when you are not quite over an illness, it is much easier if you have your sermon written out in front of you.

Extempore sermons must still be prayed about and prepared beforehand. A Methodist minister once told me the cautionary tale of another minister who said one day "I've not prepared my sermons for the last month. I've just stood up and started speaking, relying on the Holy Spirit." To which some of his congregation replied

"Well, the Holy Spirit has been a bit boring over the last month."

It is sometimes a good idea to preach extempore sermons at services with children, especially if you are going to walk down the aisle asking questions of the children, but you need to keep your sermon simple so that you can remember everything, e.g. *'Who'd like to tell me what they found under the Christmas tree or at the end of the bed when they woke up this morning? We've all had presents because today is Christmas Day. Christmas Day is Jesus' birthday. Jesus is God's present to us. It's nice to give presents back. The best present we can give back to God is ourselves.'*

7. PREPARING THE PREACHER

I normally try to read my sermon again before going to bed on Saturday night or early on Sunday morning before going to church and I say a little prayer that God will help me get my message across. If you are preaching on a weekday, find time during the day to do the same. It is very important that the whole business of preparing, writing and preaching a sermon is surrounded with prayer. Our sermons will suffer if we neglect our prayer lives and the congregation will notice it before we do.

Congregations are also very good at sniffing out any traces of hypocrisy or double standards in the preacher. An old priest I knew well once told me he had been to a service where the vicar had told the congregation in his sermon: "You must give and give, until it hurts!" Unfortunately it was well known in the parish that this particular priest was extremely mean and ungenerous, so his sermon did not ring true. The preacher is first of all addressing himself or herself, before addressing others. This means, most importantly, that we should not preach about something unless we ourselves believe it and can affirm it from the heart.

Writing is an integral part of preaching. I believe that one cannot write well unless one also reads well. Unfortunately, reading is often the first thing to be neglected under the many different pressures of parish life. Yet preaching needs to be nourished by regular reading: we shall not have any new ideas unless we feed our minds. The preacher should try to read widely. This obviously should include books on Theology and Biblical Studies, but also books on other subjects including literature, and also newspapers, magazines and periodicals. Fifteen minutes a day spent reading a good book, squeezed somehow between all the engagements of a busy diary, can make a very great difference.

Those called to the ministry of the word would do well to give some thought to their appearance: robes that need washing or dry-cleaning, dirty shoes and a generally unkempt appearance are not attractive and may suggest to some in the congregation that we do not taking preaching - or them - seriously.

Lastly, all of us who preach sermons should remind ourselves very often that we are the messengers, not the message. Our work of preaching is of very great importance but we ourselves are never indispensable: the Church of God has managed without us for two thousand years, and it will cope perfectly well without us again.

8.   PREACHING A SERMON

Those who are new to preaching are sometimes surprised by how physical a thing is delivering a sermon. You communicate your message not only with your voice but also with your eyes, facial expressions and body language. It is important that as far as possible the preacher should be visible as well as audible to the congregation.

Where is the best place for you to preach your sermon? The answer will depend on the interior of the church and the nature of the service at which you are preaching. I would suggest that it is generally best to use the pulpit for most sermons if your church has one. Pulpits were built so that the preacher could be both seen and heard, and if you preach your sermon standing at the front of the nave the people sitting at the back of the church or in the aisles or transepts may have an obscured view of you. Also, psychologically, to preach a sermon standing in front of a dusty and disused pulpit may suggest to some people in the church that the sermon is now less important than when it was delivered from the pulpit.

If you are preaching to a handful of people at a weekday Eucharist it might seem a bit silly to climb into the pulpit, especially if you are only going to preach for two or three minutes. It would be better to do so from a lectern or from the chancel steps. An extempore sermon for children is probably best delivered standing at the front of the church, which means you are free to move down the nave asking questions, etc. Addresses at

Compline can be effectively delivered from a chair in front of the altar or at the end of the nave, depending on where the congregation are sitting.

Having carefully prepared a sermon, it is important that the congregation can hear you deliver it. If there is a hymn before you preach do not join in singing it but rest your voice, even if it is only for a minute. Many churches are equipped with microphones and sound systems which are a very great help especially if you are contending with a sore throat. Whether you have a microphone or not, try to spot someone sitting at the back of the church and say to yourself "I'm going to make sure that lady in the blue coat hears every word." Just as important as speaking loudly is speaking clearly: there is not much point in projecting your voice if you mumble your words and the congregation strain to make sense of what you are saying. It will be very helpful if a glass of water can be placed within easy reach and if you have a handkerchief in your pocket in case you suffer a coughing fit.

The presentation of a sermon can make all the difference and can raise a mediocre sermon a notch or two. Listen to several different radio stations and note carefully how the announcers use their voices. Do not simply read your text aloud from the pulpit. If you are reading a quotation, lift up your voice a note or two to signify that it is a quotation. Try to avoid dropping or raising the inflection of your voice at the end of every sentence. If you can preach your sermon at the 8.00 a.m. Eucharist it will be a bit better and more natural when you repeat it at 10.00 a.m.

It is important to maintain eye contact with the congregation when preaching. Do not jerk about like a jack-in-a-box in the pulpit but turn around from time to time to let your eye range over the whole congregation, and do not forget to look at the choir and servers occasionally.

Archbishop Lang - himself a very gifted orator - used to describe certain priests who worked very hard to befriend people in their parishes and to get them to come to church. When these newcomers were finally persuaded to attend a service they found that their jovial and caring parish priest had become transformed in the pulpit into a stiff and unnatural figure who addressed them in an odd and strangulated way. It sometimes took considerable effort to persuade them to return a second time. Lang concluded that that preacher should try to aim for the manner of a friend talking to friends about things that were important to them both.

When you first start to preach you will feel nervous and you will be a bit stiff and strangulated like Archbishop Lang's priest. With experience you will overcome your nerves, though every now and then they will return when you have to deal with a sensitive topic or to preach at a difficult occasion. This is no bad thing because it shows that we have not become over-confident or blasé about preaching. With practice you will develop a style of preaching of your own. Remember, you cannot be another Wesley, Spurgeon, Newman or Edward King, even if you wanted to: you can only be yourself, and if you are not yourself in the pulpit your sermons will not ring true.

Try not to preach when you are over-tired, though this is not easy if it is your third service on Sunday morning or you are preaching in the evening after a busy day. Never lose your temper in the pulpit. The exhausted priest who blurts out "Oh, you silly people!" may blow away in seconds the effects of years of careful work in the parish. We all have strong views about various subjects and extra vigilance is needed when we speak about them in our sermons. We may, for example, care passionately about exploitation and poverty in the third world, but ranting and raving about them in a sermon may be counter-productive and will not be nearly so effective as two or three carefully crafted sentences, calmly delivered.

9. PREACHING AT BAPTISMS, MARRIAGES AND FUNERAL SERVICES

Although this work is mainly about preaching on Sundays I thought I would add something about preaching at Baptisms, Marriages and Funeral services which is rather a specialised subject.

The crucial thing about preaching at Baptisms, Marriages and Funerals is to try to convey to the people concerned that they matter and that you care about them. It may be your third wedding that Saturday or your fourth funeral that week and you may be feeling very weary, but for the parents of the baby being Baptised, the couple being married or the bereaved relatives at the funeral, the service is a unique occasion which they may well remember for the rest of their lives. Their understanding of Christianity may be extremely patchy and their motives may be mixed but we should always remember that *they* have still approached the Church at this juncture in their lives - the Holy Spirit may have been working overtime to get them there - and it is up to us to welcome them and to make the most of this opportunity to tell them something about Jesus. Try to preach at Baptisms, Marriages and Funerals as though it is the only thing that matters that day.

BAPTISMS

You will probably know the family of the baby to be baptised, at least by sight. You may have visited them at home or seen them during parish Baptism preparation sessions. Try in the short time available to strike up a rapport with them and to convey to them, firstly, that Baptism is very wonderful and important, and secondly, that you are greatly looking forward to Baptising their baby. If the parents are not regular churchgoers they may well be a bit nervous, unsure about the reaction of their families and friends to sitting through a church service, and perhaps a little afraid of somehow being 'brainwashed' by the Church. Many parents will promise all sorts of things to get their baby baptised and then never darken the door of the church again, or at least not until the birth of their next baby. But having a baby *does* cause many people to think about the direction of their lives and what matters to them and there have been some families in every parish I have worked in who have come to faith because of the impact of a Baptism. A good sermon can make a big difference.

If the Baptism is to take place during a Sung Eucharist on a Sunday morning the preacher has two options. The first is to preach about the sacrament of Baptism. It is doubtless a good idea to do this once a year to remind the congregation about their own Baptisms, but the congregation may rebel if they get a sermon about Baptism every first Sunday of the month or whenever you hold your Baptisms. The second option is to preach about the appointed readings. Remember, though, that there will be a number of people in the congregation who have come just for the Baptism and who are not used to being in church or to church services. Keep your sermon simple and short, see if you can weave something about Baptism into it and try to mention the names of the children to be baptised.

If you are preaching at a special Baptism service, perhaps at 3.00 p.m. on Sunday, it is best just to talk about the sacrament of Baptism. Once again, keep it simple and short. Talk about the Baptism of Jesus in the river Jordan by John the Baptist and about our being baptised into the death and resurrection of Christ. Explain that Baptism is the beginning of a pilgrimage through life to God and make it clear that the baby will need the prayers, help and encouragement of the parents and godparents. You will have explained this already during the Baptism preparation session but it will not do them any harm to hear it again in church. See if you can manage a reference to Confirmation. If you are stuck for an idea, try saying something about the water, the font, the baptismal oil or the paschal candle. I have often found that just as important as the sermon are a few words of explanation here and there during the Baptism. If you are also the person baptising the baby, do try to look as though you are enjoying it, even if the baby weighs a ton, has been sick down your robes and is now bawling into your ear.

MARRIAGE

The new *Common Worship* marriage service requires a sermon at a wedding, though this can and probably should be quite brief. Much of what I have said about preaching at Baptisms also applies to preaching at Marriages. You will have a church full of people, many of whom are unfamiliar with church services. The families of the bride and groom can sometimes work themselves into a dreadful state of nerves and make mountains out of molehills before a wedding. The bride and groom will perhaps be a bit nervous about getting their words right and putting on the wedding ring. You must appear perfectly calm and pleased to see them in your church, and you must not be put off if the photographer is doing something you have asked him not to do or some of the congregation are noisily whispering or giggling. You must concentrate on helping the bride and groom to get off to the best possible start in their married life.

There will normally be a reading from the Bible before the sermon. Try to encourage the bride and groom to choose something suitable. The wedding at Cana is particularly appropriate and can be used to make the point that if the first miracle Christ performed as a sign of his divinity was at a wedding, then in God's eyes marriage must be important.

It is a good idea to remind the congregation that Christian marriage is a vocation from God, a way of life to which He has called the bride and groom and in which they will seek and serve their Lord. Their marriage vows unite them for better, for worse, for richer, for poorer, in sickness and in health, until death parts them. This is an awesome undertaking, but God who has brought them together will help and support them in the years ahead if they will let Him.

A word of caution, though: I have never forgotten the second wedding at which I assisted after being ordained a deacon when the preacher was a visiting clergyman. He droned on about the ups and downs of married life, the couple not really knowing one another, it not being a bed of roses, etc., until the poor, nervous bride burst into tears, much to the consternation of her groom. The preacher produced a handkerchief for her from his cassock pocket and carried on in the same vein. Some topics are best dealt with in a different way at marriage preparation sessions and not during the wedding sermon.

I find it good to address quite a bit of the sermon directly to the bride and groom in order to make it more personal. If you are going to write out or print your sermon for each wedding, it is a nice idea to present it to the bride and groom afterwards with the suggestion that they might like to read it on their wedding anniversary to remind them of the day.

On the whole I am inclined to think that the hallmarks of a good wedding sermon are that it mentions God, is realistic, celebratory, and above all encouraging.

FUNERAL SERVICES

Until the twentieth century most Church of England funeral services were burials. The priest just read the service from the Prayer Book and the body was buried. There was seldom a sermon. Patterns of mourning were changed very greatly by the widespread bereavement occasioned by the First World War and later in the century by the growth in popularity of cremation. Most families would nowadays expect the officiant to say something at a funeral service and I have often come away from funerals with the impression that the sermon was the most important part of it for the mourners. Funerals are sometimes very taxing for the officiant, especially if the deceased has died in tragic circumstances, and the expectations placed upon the sermon can add to the burden. At the same time a funeral sermon is an opportunity to help a family at a very difficult time in their lives and very gently to say something about the Good News of Christ. In many instances the family may not know what they believe in, but it is important to them that the officiant is a man or woman of faith.

The best advice ever given to me about funerals came from an undertaker when I was at theological college. "Most people", he said, "come to a funeral to hear something nice said about the deceased." From this I learnt the important lesson that if you start your sermon by saying something about the deceased - remembering that this is not an exercise in hagiography - you will gain the attention of the congregation and you can then go on to say something about the Crucifixion, Resurrection and our hope of eternal life in Christ.

Try to visit the next-of-kin before the funeral in order to find out something about the deceased. No two pre-funeral visits are the same: in one house you will be shown the door after twenty minutes, whilst in another you will be struggling to get away after two hours. Listen very carefully to all that is said and try to behave in such a way that the family feel confident to tell you if there are any problems. If you discover that the deceased beat up his wife and children and spent his money in the pub and betting shop, his family will have very mixed feelings now he is dead and it will not help them if you tell everyone that he was a perfect husband and father who will be grievously missed. It would be better to say "Mary, Edward and Elizabeth and everyone here today will have their own thoughts and memories of Henry going back many years," and then move on to say something about his career and hobbies. Listen out carefully, too, in case the family have recently suffered another bereavement.

If you cannot arrange to see the next-of-kin, try to talk to them on the telephone, though this is seldom as good as a face-to-face meeting. If the next-of-kin did not know the deceased very well, see what you can find out from his or her neighbours, or perhaps the warden if he or she lived in a warden-controlled flat. If all else fails, get to the church or crematorium in good time and see what you can find out from any of the mourners who have turned up early.

You will most likely not have met the deceased yourself but do not say so in your sermon. Neither should you say, "*I am told* William loved horses" or whatever: it is a tremendous turn-off. If you did meet the deceased, however briefly, say so: "I remember meeting Eleanor at the luncheon club, which she used to enjoy so greatly." This will mean a lot to the family.

If you are stuck for something to say, use a sentence such as "Everyone here today will have their own special memories of Matilda. Perhaps it was the time when she helped you out on a bad day, or said something to cheer you up at a very difficult time in your life. Perhaps only you and she knew about it." You will be surprised how often people nod at this.

Try to mention briefly the names of the deceased's immediate relations (you might want to include them by name in the prayer for those who mourn), his or her career and hobbies. Do not be afraid to allude to a long illness before death: it will have been a big part in the lives of the next-of-kin, who may be exhausted with nursing.

If the deceased was a practising Christian, give thanks that the pilgrimage started in Baptism is now completed and that they have gone home. If the funeral is in church and the deceased was a regular communicant, you might like to point out that he or she received Holy Communion here every Sunday but has now moved into the nearer presence of God where sacraments are not needed.

It is a good idea at all funerals to make a passing reference to sinfulness: "Like all of us, Stephen had his sins and failings, which we now leave up to the Lord to sort out." That will suffice. There may well be someone in the congregation who was deeply hurt by the deceased. You do not want the funeral service to make things worse for them, and you hope that a reference to sinfulness and our need of God's forgiveness might help them to draw a line under the experience and to move on.

Having got the attention of the congregation you can move on to talk about eternal life. I find it best to talk very simply about the Easter story: at such moments people can more easily take in a story than abstract ideas. Sometimes you may be asked to take the funeral of someone who led a very unchristian life or who was an atheist or agnostic. You can still talk about our *hope* of eternal life: God knows each of us better than we know ourselves, we are all sinners in need His mercy and He will decide whom to admit to heaven. Your primary task is to help the mourners, not to lay extra burdens on top of their grief.

After a while you will develop the confidence to preach from brief notes about the life of the deceased, though you may find it helpful to have a 'standard' funeral sermon printed out on paper in front of you. Your sermon should be brief. If the funeral is at a crematorium you may only have twenty minutes for the whole service. If you use notes, write the name of the deceased in large letters at the top so you do not get it wrong.

From time to time we all have to preach at the funerals of people who have died in tragic circumstances. This can be very taxing, especially if you have a church full of very upset people. Write your sermon out in full: do not rely on notes in case you lose your thread under the emotion of the moment and are left floundering. You may find it helpful to begin by saying something like "Since we heard of Kathleen's tragic and untimely death, I am sure that all sorts of questions have been going through our minds. It isn't easy to point to all the answers today. Instead, we have come here to give thanks for Kathleen's life, to help ourselves and one another with our grief at her death, and in our prayers to commend her soul into the hands of our loving, heavenly Father."

If the deceased died an untimely death, it may be helpful to point out that it does not matter how long we live, but how we spend our time on earth: some people dying aged 45 may have given and received far more that other people dying at 90.

If you have to preach at the funeral of a child, try to arrange for someone else to drive you to and from the funeral in case you feel overcome afterwards. Write your sermon out in full and keep it brief and simple.

For many centuries the Church would not grant Christian burial to those who 'laid violent hands upon themselves', on the grounds that suicide was believed to be a rejection of God. We now understand that suicide is often the result of an illness. Such a bereavement is particularly hard for the family to bear. You might find it helpful to say something such as "For many years Malcolm must have been weighed down by a very heavy burden, of which we perhaps knew nothing. Today, in the midst of our sadness, we give thanks that this heavy burden has been taken from his shoulders." We should always remember that death and judgement are, as much as anything, about healing.

The content of a funeral sermon is very important, but perhaps more important still is the way in which we say it. This may be your second or third funeral that day, but for the family it is a unique, emotional day which they will remember decades afterwards. Preaching at funerals is often very draining, but when it goes well one is very grateful and humbled afterwards to have been used by God to help people at a difficult time in their lives.

10.   REACTIONS TO SERMONS

Members of the congregation will sometimes say *"Oh, that was a marvellous sermon!"* It may well have been, but equally all this may mean is that you have entertained them. The absence of a reaction does not mean it was a bad sermon, merely that your words are still soaking in. Sometimes people will remember a throw-away remark or an illustration and miss your main point. The test of a good Sunday sermon is how much the congregation can remember of it after lunch.

From time to time there will be someone in the congregation who hears you incorrectly or who gets the wrong end of the stick. Try to explain your point again calmly and succinctly: the church porch after a service is not the best place for raised voices. It may help to show them your text if they have worked themselves up into a state. Ask yourself afterwards whether you might have preached more plainly, but do not upset yourself if you have done nothing wrong. You may have got it in the neck because the person is unhappy about something completely different, and there are also some people who regrettably seem to enjoy feeling offended.

People do not learn Christianity systematically and you will frequently discover that people who have been coming to church for years have great gaps in their understanding and will suddenly be taken aback by what you regard as very elementary points. Do not appear surprised when they say something to you. You will also find that you labour away for years to teach something with no success, and then someone else preaches and people begin to grasp it. Do not be jealous of other preachers: they have their bad days and failures too. Most people will be very grateful for your sermons but will not be very good about telling you.

11.   CONCLUSION

I would suggest that there are four things necessary for good preaching:

1.   A love of Christ and sense of excitement about the Good News.

2.   A love of the people listening to your sermon and the belief that they and their lives matter.

3.   A love of words.

4.   The ability to have a good laugh at yourself.

There is only one way to learn how to preach and that is to get on and do it. So long as you do not preach heresy, it does not matter if some of your early sermons are not too good so long as you are open to learning from your experiences. Inevitably, you will preach both good and bad sermons: you may be unwell or under a great deal of pressure and this will have an effect on your preaching, but strive to do your best and do not preach second rate sermons when you can do better with a little more preparation. It is hard work writing a sermon every week but never undervalue the importance of regularly feeding and guiding your people from the pulpit week after week.

Above all, rely on the Holy Spirit. If you have asked Him to guide you, He will also be at work amongst your congregation. We will most likely never be aware of some of the most powerful things God uses our sermons to convey to our hearers. Words from the pulpit burrow deep in our minds and we sometimes recall them years afterwards. Never underestimate the power or the importance of a sermon.